EXPLORING THE WORLD

CARTIER

Jacques Cartier in Search of the Northwest Passage

BY JEAN F. BLASHFIELD

Content Adviser: Professor Sherry L. Field, Department of Social Science Education,
College of Education, The University of Georgia

Reading Adviser: Dr. Linda D. Labbo, Department of Reading Education,
College of Education, The University of Georgia

COMPASS POINT BOOKS
MINNEAPOLIS, MINNESOTA

Compass Point Books
3722 West 50th Street, #115
Minneapolis, MN 55410

Visit Compass Point Books on the Internet at *www.compasspointbooks.com* or
e-mail your request to *custserv@compasspointbooks.com*

Photographs ©: Stock Montage, cover, 1, 2 (background), 12 (top), 21, 39, 44; Visual Language
Library, cover (background), 42 (background), 43 (background), 45 (background); North Wind
Picture Archives, back cover, 4, 7, 13, 14, 17, 18, 19 (top), 22, 25, 27, 28, 33, 37, 41;
Bettmann/Corbis, 5, 24, 46–47; Photri-Microstock, 6, 15 (bottom); Hulton Getty/Archive Photos, 8,
19 (bottom), 20; Nik Wheeler/Corbis, 10, 40; Marc Garanger/Corbis, 11; Francis G. Mayer/Corbis,
12 (bottom); Robert McCaw, 15 (top), 31; Unicorn Stock Photos, 16; Dave G. Houser/Corbis, 23;
Paul A. Souders/Corbis, 26, 35; The Purcell Team/Corbis, 29; Erwin C. "Bud" Nielson/Visual
Unlimited, 30; Robert Estall/Corbis, 32; Historical Picture Archive/Corbis, 34; Rob Simpson/Visuals
Unlimited, 36; John Heseltine/Corbis, 38.

Editors: E. Russell Primm, Emily J. Dolbear, and Melissa McDaniel
Photo Researcher: Svetlana Zhurkina
Photo Selector: Catherine Neitge
Designer: Design Lab
Cartographer: XNR Productions, Inc.

Library of Congress Cataloging-in-Publication Data
    Blashfield, Jean F.
    Cartier : Jacques Cartier in search of the Northwest Passage / by Jean F. Blashfield.
        p. cm. — (Exploring the world)
    Includes bibliographical references and index.
    ISBN 0-7565-0122-9 (lib. bdg.)
        1. Cartier, Jacques, 1491-1557—Juvenile literature. 2. Explorers—America—Biography—
Juvenile literature. 3. Explorers—France—Biography—Juvenile literature. 4. Canada—Discovery
and exploration—Juvenile literature. 5. Canada—History—To 1763 (New France)—Juvenile litera-
ture. 6. Northwest Passage—Discovery and exploration—French—Juvenile literature. [1. Cartier,
Jacques, 1491-1557. 2. Explorers. 3. Canada—Discovery and exploration—French. 4. Canada—
History—To 1763 (New France) 5. Northwest Passage.] I. Title. II. Series.
    E133.C3 B58 2002
    971.01'13—dc21   2001001509

Table of Contents

After Columbus

When Italian explorer Christopher Columbus sailed across the Atlantic Ocean in 1492, he thought he had discovered a new route to Asia.

Instead, he had stumbled into the Americas. He claimed the lands for the king and queen of Spain.

Spain soon grew wealthy

The three ships of Christopher Columbus

by stealing gold from the people who lived in Central and South America. Other European kings wanted some of the riches to be found in the Americas, so they sent their own explorers to claim land. The man who claimed much of what is now eastern Canada for France was Jacques Cartier.

Jacques Cartier claimed much of eastern Canada for France.

Cartier was born in 1491 in Brittany, a **peninsula** in northwestern France that juts out into the Atlantic Ocean. Living along the coast, Brittany's people, called Bretons, depended on the sea for their livelihoods. Some of them became well-known **navigators** because they knew how to find their way, or navigate, across the seas. Cartier, one of the best navigators, lived in St-Malo, on the northern coast of Brittany.

Cartier grew up in Brittany in northwestern France.

The Grand Banks

In 1497, King Henry VII of England had sent an Italian navigator named Giovanni Caboto—known to the English as John Cabot—to claim lands for England. Cabot sailed across the Atlantic and along the coast of a large island now called Newfoundland. After he returned to England, Cabot told King

John Cabot landed in what is now called Newfoundland.

Cod fishing in the Grand Banks

Henry that the western Atlantic held vast numbers of cod and other fish.

To the fishermen of Brittany, cod was more important than unexplored lands or the chance of finding gold. They headed to the area Cabot had explored off Newfoundland, which is now called the Grand Banks.

Young Breton boys often went to the Grand Banks each spring to fish with their fathers. During these trips, they learned the business of fishing and the art and science of sailing a ship. One of these boys was Jacques Cartier.

As a teenager, Jacques wondered about the mountains and

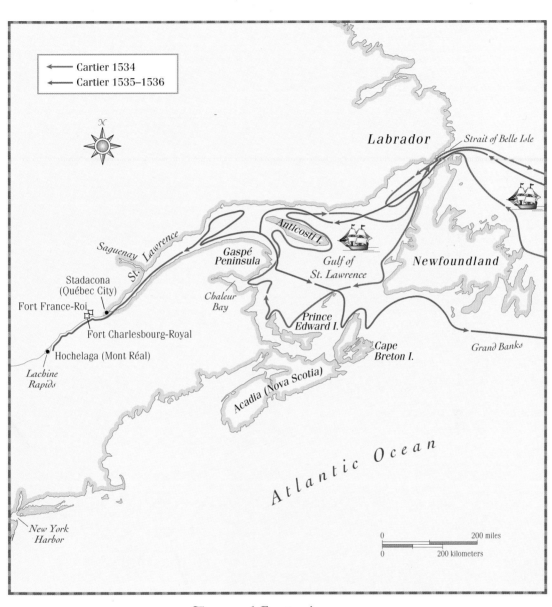

A map of Cartier's voyages

rocky cliffs he saw on the land that bordered the Grand Banks. He urged his father to take a closer look, but his father was interested only in catching fish, not in exploring unknown places.

As the years passed, fishermen sometimes sought shelter in the natural harbors and bays along the coast of Newfoundland. They didn't go inland though—their eyes were on the fish, seals, birds, and whales. Native people who lived in the coastal regions also hunted these animals, so European fishermen began to come into contact with the native people. While nothing is recorded about these meetings, the fishermen probably traded some European goods, such as iron tools, for furs.

The coastline of Newfoundland's Bonne Bay

The Making of a Navigator

Little is known about Jacques Cartier's life in France. All historians have to go on are clues from other explorers' writings and from records in St-Malo. Cartier married Catherine des Granches in 1519, but there is no record that they raised a family.

Cartier probably studied navigation at a naval school in Dieppe, in northern France. By 1524, he was skilled enough to accompany Giovanni da Verrazano, an Italian navigator who worked for France, on an **expedition** along the coast of North America. On that journey, Cartier and the other

A flag bearing the town's coat of arms flies from the tower of St-Malo castle.

crew members became the first Europeans to see New York harbor.

In the hunt for gold, it is possible that Cartier also traveled to South America and visited the coast of Brazil. He gained no wealth, but his **reputation** as an excellent navigator was growing.

Meanwhile, King Francis I of France decided that his country should become more involved in the exploration of the Americas. He asked Admiral Philippe de Chabot, Lord de Brion, of the French navy to arrange an expedition.

At that time, spices from Asia, such as nutmeg and cloves, were popular in Europe and were valuable trade items. To get the spices, European ships had to travel all the way around the southern tip of Africa

Giovanni da Verrazano

King Francis I

and across the Indian Ocean to the Molucca islands where the spices grew. (The Moluccas were once called the Spice Islands.) The French king hoped that someone— preferably a Frenchman— would find a water route across the Americas—a

This woodcut illustrated a 1549 cookbook. Spices used in European cooking came from Asia.

"Northwest Passage." Such a water route would allow ships to travel quickly from Europe to the Pacific Ocean, reaching the Spice Islands from the other direction.

The First Voyage

Because of Cartier's reputation as a navigator, Brion asked him to lead the expedition. With two ships and a crew of sixty-one men, Cartier left France on April 20, 1534. About three weeks later, the group reached the rocky coast of North America that Cartier had wondered about when he was young.

Cartier and his crew left St-Malo in April 1534.

Cartier's first stop was an island off the coast of Newfoundland. French fishermen already knew this area well. Cartier then turned north and swung around the island of Newfoundland. He sailed through the Strait of Belle Isle, a narrow waterway that separates Newfoundland from the Canadian mainland, and into the Gulf of St. Lawrence. During the voyage, Cartier sketched maps and gave names to many places. He claimed the coastal lands he saw for France.

Heading south, Cartier curved along Prince Edward Island and the coast of New

Top: a view across the narrow Strait of Belle Isle in Newfoundland. Bottom: the coastline of Prince Edward Island

Perce Rock stands on the shore of the Gaspé Peninsula.

Returning to open water, he landed on the northern shore of the bay, on the Gaspé Peninsula. There he first saw the native people who lived in the area. They were probably Huron Indians.

The Indians came to the peninsula to fish and catch seals. They lived in the village of Stadacona on the cliff above the St. Lawrence River, now the site of Québec City.

Brunswick. He entered Chaleur Bay, thinking it might be the Northwest Passage. But the river that emptied into the bay was little more than a stream.

The Europeans in their work clothes and boots studied the brown-skinned natives in paint and furs. For two days, the groups eyed each other. Then Donnacona, the chief of the Indian fishermen, indicated that the strangers could come on shore from their ships. His people gave the Europeans some of their food, but Cartier's men did not like the taste of it.

The Indians and the Europeans communicated as best they could, but it was difficult because they spoke different languages. The Indians called their village *kanata*, but Cartier thought the word referred to the whole area, so the entire region became known as *Canada.*

On July 24, 1534, Donnacona watched in alarm as the strangers erected a huge wooden object on the shore. He did not know that it was a Christian cross, but he understood that the cross and the flying banner (the flag of King Francis I) meant that the white men were claiming the land.

When Donnacona objected, however, Cartier said that the wooden cross was only a marker to help him find the spot again.

Donnacona was

Cartier and Donnacona

Cartier claims the land for France.

France with him. The chief watched as the ship carrying his sons disappeared beyond the horizon, not certain whether he would ever see them again.

Back home in France, Cartier reported to Brion and the king. He described the places he had seen and the people he had met. He said that the rocky coast north of the Strait of Belle Isle was so terrible that it could only belong to Cain, the biblical character who killed his brother Abel. Ever since, the Labrador coast, as this region is now called, has been known as "the land God gave to Cain."

even more alarmed when Cartier insisted that Donnacona's sons— Domagaya and Taignoagny— board his ship and return to

Little is known about the Indian brothers' winter in France. They must have found

Islands at the mouth of the St. Lawrence River

everything strange and confusing, but they worked at learning the French language so that they could **interpret** for their people, and they told Cartier about a great river— a river so long that no one had seen its end. Cartier convinced the king that the river might be the Northwest Passage, and the king agreed to fund another expedition.

Jacques Cartier

Return Visit

On May 19, 1535, Cartier set sail for Canada again. This time his expedition included three ships—the *Grande Hermine,* the *Petite Hermine,* and the *Émérillon*—and 100 men, as well as the two young Indians.

After a journey plagued by spring storms, Cartier again sailed through the Strait of Belle Isle. This time he named the gulf behind the island of Newfoundland. He called it the Gulf of St. Lawrence because his ships reached it on August 10, the feast day of Saint Lawrence.

Cartier sights land.

Cartier's ships sailed up the river to Stadacona.

The young Huron boys directed Cartier into the great river that emptied into the gulf. In later years, the river too would be given the name St. Lawrence. The Indians led Cartier upriver to their home village of Stadacona. When they arrived, they had bad news for their father. They told him that in the strange land across the sea where they had been, it was believed that the land of the Hurons now belonged to France.

In the days that followed, Cartier heard tales of the "Kingdom of Saguenay," which was supposedly filled with gold and jewels. Cartier talked of going beyond Stadacona, hoping

*Donnacona and his sons dressed up as devils
to warn Cartier not to sail beyond the village.*

that he might find this rich land. But Donnacona was alarmed, and he warned Cartier not to go beyond Stadacona. The chief and his sons put on a perform-ance as devils to show Cartier that evil beings lived upriver. Nevertheless Cartier refused to heed their warnings.

Cartier and thirty-two men took the *Émérillon* (the smallest of his ships) and several **longboats** upriver. The expedition members left behind were instructed to build a fort to serve as their winter quarters.

The Royal Mountain

As Cartier sailed upriver, he saw land that was fertile and lush, even in autumn. Eventually, the water became so shallow that the *Émérillon* could go no farther. Cartier and his men continued on in the longboats.

On October 2, they reached a large island. Hundreds of people greeted him with what Cartier said were "great signs of

Huge metal monuments at the Musée de la Gaspésie commemorate the landing of Cartier on the Gaspé Peninsula.

joy." After a night of feasts and dancing, they led Cartier and his men several miles along a trail past fields of crops to a large town they called Hochelaga. The town was protected by three rows of wooden stakes. Perhaps the people of Hochelaga had protected their town because they had enemies. Perhaps the Hurons of Stadacona were their enemies, and these were the people Donnacona had warned Cartier about.

The town consisted of about fifty houses, each large enough for several families. An outdoor fire was used for cooking, and the townspeople ate outside. Cartier noted that when the

Cartier meets the people of Hochelaga

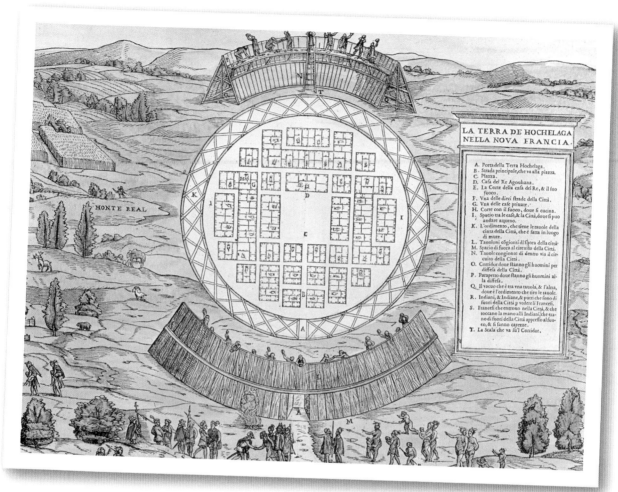

An early illustration of Hochelaga

people of Hochelaga gathered together, they smoked a dried leaf. Europeans later called this leaf tobacco.

Hochelaga lay in the shadow of a hill, which Cartier called *Mont Réal*, meaning "Royal Mountain." From Hochelaga, the forested hill may have seemed like a mountain, but it was only

The city of Montreal today as seen from the summit of Mont-Royal

about 730 feet (222 meters) high. The hill, originally called Mont Réal, and the city that grew around it are now known as Montreal.

Although the Indians and the Frenchmen could not understand each other's languages, they were friendly. About 1,500 Hochelagan people performed a ritual dance for Cartier and his men that lasted through the night. Cartier wrote that the ceremony was "as good a welcome as ever a father gave to his son." In exchange, Cartier gave the villagers many small European items, such as beads and hatchets.

Today, no one knows for sure who the Hochelagans were. Their language

A 1609 map depicts Hochelaga.

was related to Iroquois, a family of languages spoken by Indians in eastern North America. But

their way of life was different from the other people who spoke Iroquois languages. The

Cartier on the top of Mont Réal

Cartier looked west to a rough spot in the river, where the water flowed over rocks as it quickly dropped in **elevation.** Cartier realized that large ships would never be able to travel over those rapids. His hopes of finding the North-west Passage had again been dashed.

More than one hundred years later, another explorer, René-Robert Cavalier, Sieur de La Salle, called the rapids *La petite Chine,* meaning "Little China." Today, this stretch of the St. Lawrence River is known as the Lachine Rapids.

Hochelagan **civilization** may have vanished with their large village. From atop Mont Réal,

Fireworks explode over the Jacques Cartier Bridge, which spans the St. Lawrence River in Montreal.

The Terrible Winter

Cartier and his men returned to Stadacona, where their wooden fort was now built. They moved their supplies and stoves from their ships into the fort and prepared to spend the winter.

Snow covers the Isles de la Madeleine in the Gulf of St. Lawrence. In Canada, winters are much more severe than those in France.

Tea made from the bark and needles of the white cedar is said to have cured Cartier and his men of scurvy.

France has rather mild winters, so Cartier and his men were completely unprepared for the hard Canadian winter. They were also hit hard by diseases that would eventually kill one-fourth of them. Perhaps the worst was scurvy, a disease caused by lack of vitamin C. When scurvy struck, the men's gums swelled, causing their teeth to fall out. Their joints became sore. Gradually, their blood vessels tore, allowing their blood to leak out, and the men died in pain.

Some stories say that Domagaya, one of Donnacona's sons, told the French that they could cure scurvy by making tea

The village of Tadoussac lies at the head of the St. Lawrence and Saguenay Rivers where Cartier landed in 1535.

from the bark and needles of a white cedar evergreen tree, which the Indians called the anneda. The Frenchmen followed Domagaya's advice, and their group survived the winter. Cartier himself apparently kept the survivors' spirits high.

When spring came, Cartier repaid the Indians' kindness by again kidnapping the chief's sons, along with Donnacona himself and seven other Indians. He wanted to take them back to France so that they could tell the king directly about the Kingdom of Saguenay and the treasure that might be found in Canada.

The Years Pass in France

Back in France, however, the king was now at war with Spain, and he was much too busy to pay attention to Cartier. Meanwhile, the explorer apparently tried to keep the Indians healthy, but the strange food and **environment** took their toll. Eventually all of the Indians died, except one little girl.

Cartier's house in France

King Francis I

As the war with Spain raged on, the king realized he would need more money to keep fighting. He remembered that Cartier thought there might be gold in Canada. The king decided to start a **colony** in Canada. The colonists could then search for gold.

The king chose Cartier to lead the colonizing expedition.

He wrote that he had "confidence in the character, judgment, ability, loyalty, hardihood, great diligence, and experience of Jacques Cartier." But then he put a **nobleman** named Jean-François de La Roque, Sieur de Roberval, in charge of the colony, naming him governor-general.

Cartier did not like Roberval to begin with. He liked him even less as the months passed and Roberval's ships were still not ready for the voyage to Canada. Cartier then asked permission to leave ahead of Roberval. On May 23, 1541, Cartier departed from St-Malo with five ships, enough supplies to last two years, and more than 1,000 crew members and colonists. Many of the colonists were prisoners.

The Roberval Colony

Cartier and the colonists arrived in Canada after a stormy three-month voyage. This time the Hurons no longer trusted Cartier and did not make the Europeans feel welcome. Cartier sailed up the St. Lawrence River to what is now Cap Rouge and built a fort for the winter.

When spring arrived, Cartier

Atlantic Ocean waves crash onto the rocky coast of Newfoundland.

and the surviving colonists and crew headed back toward Newfoundland. There they found the Roberval group, who had left France only two months before. Roberval had come with 200 people, both prisoners and entire high-born families, including men, women, and children.

Roberval demanded that Cartier and his men turn around and go back to Hochelaga with him, but Cartier knew that his crew was not willing to spend another winter there. He told Roberval that the Indians were no longer friendly, but Roberval refused to listen. Unwilling to be second-in-command to such a man, Cartier and his men sailed away during the night.

Roberval's group continued up the St. Lawrence River and found the abandoned fort. They rebuilt it and gave it a new name—France-Roi. Then Roberval sent

Cartier found Roberval's group in Newfoundland.

his ships back to France for more supplies. He was certain that his colonists could easily survive the winter.

When winter arrived, however, their experience was no better than Cartier's had been. In fact, conditions were even worse because Roberval was a cruel man. Anyone who disobeyed him was brutally whipped. Some colonists were even executed.

By spring, more than half the colonists had died. When Roberval's ships returned from France, the remaining colonists left Canada and headed for home.

Roberval had not only failed to establish a colony, but the "treasure" he brought back

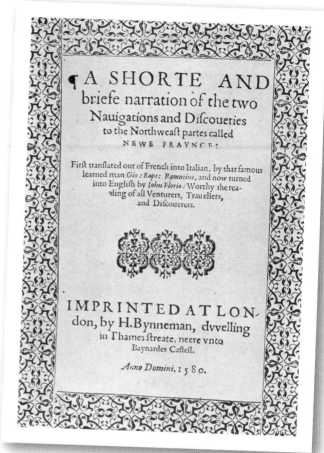

An account of Cartier's trips was published in 1580.

for the king turned out to be worthless. What he thought was gold was actually fool's gold, an iron mineral. And the "diamonds" were quartz crystals.

The Future Cartier Made

After failing to establish the colony, Cartier himself returned to St-Malo, where he lived out his life as a businessman. He died in 1557. He had gained no wealth as a result of his voyages, but France had gained possession of a land many times larger than itself.

Cartier's treatment of the

A statue of Jacques Cartier in St-Malo

Indian people of Canada guaranteed that white men would never again be met by smiles and dancing. Historian Georges Sioui wrote, "The arrogance of Cartier, who didn't bother to ask the Indians' permission to explore their territory or to settle there, offended the Indians."

Samuel de Champlain

By the time another French explorer, Samuel de Champlain, reached Hochelaga in 1603, no trace remained of the large town that Cartier had visited. It is possible that Cartier's and Roberval's crews had carried diseases, such as smallpox, that wiped out the Indians.

Not until 1605 did the French again try to colonize the vast land they claimed as New France. Led by Champlain, the colonists settled Nova Scotia, creating the first permanent European settlement in North America north of Florida.

The St. Lawrence River runs through Québec City.

Cartier ignored Canada's real treasure—furs.

In 1609, Champlain sailed into the St. Lawrence River and established a colony that he called Québec. The St. Lawrence River itself eventually became part of the border between Canada and the United States.

The fabled Kingdom of Saguenay was never found. Gold was eventually discovered in Canada, but hundreds of years later and thousands of miles away from where Cartier had explored. In his search for gold, Cartier had ignored the wealth in furs that was Canada's real treasure. It would be the quest for furs, not gold, that would bring Europeans to this great land.

Glossary

civilization a highly developed and organized society

colony a territory settled by people from another country and controlled by that country

elevation height above sea level

environment the natural and social conditions of an area

expedition a long journey taken for a special purpose; the group of people making that journey

interpret to explain in a different language

longboats large boats moved by many rowers

navigators people who use maps, compasses, and the stars to travel the seas by ship

nobleman a person from a high-ranking family

peninsula an area of land that is almost completely surrounded by water

reputation a person's character as judged by other people

Did You Know?

- On his first voyage, Cartier crossed the Atlantic in only twenty days.

- When he sailed from France to Canada, Cartier was looking for a water route to China.

- Cartier was so impressed with the white cedar, which cured his men of scurvy, that he took specimens of it back to France. It was the first native American tree transplanted to Europe and became known as the arborvitae–the tree of life.

- The name Montreal comes from *Mont Réal,* or "Royal Mountain," the name Cartier gave the hill.

Important Dates in Cartier's Life

1491
Jacques Cartier born in St-Malo, France

1524
Accompanies Giovanni da Verrazano on a voyage to North America

1534
Leads a voyage to Canada; returns to France

1536
Returns to France

1542
Returns to France for the last time

1557
Dies in St-Malo

1541
Sails to Canada again

1519
Marries Catherine des Granches

1535
Leads a second voyage to Canada

Important People

GIOVANNI CABOTO (C.1450–C.1499) Italian navigator who sailed to Newfoundland and explored the Grand Banks; known to the English as John Cabot

LORD DE BRION PHILIPPE DE CHABOT (1480–1543) admiral in the French navy who arranged for Cartier's expedition to the Americas

SAMUEL DE CHAMPLAIN (C.1567–1635) French explorer who led the colonization of Nova Scotia

CHRISTOPHER COLUMBUS (1451–1506) an Italian explorer who claimed the Americas for Spain

DONNACONA (?) chief of the Indians living in Stadacona when Cartier explored Canada; father of Domagaya and Taignoagny

FRANCIS I (1494–1547) king of France who encouraged the exploration of the Americas

RENÉ-ROBERT CAVALIER, SIEUR DE LA SALLE (1643–1687) French explorer who traveled through Canada and down the Mississippi River; claimed the Louisiana Territory for France

JEAN-FRANÇOIS DE LA ROQUE, SIEUR DE ROBERVAL (1500–1561) French nobleman who failed to establish a colony on the land explored by Cartier

GIOVANNI DA VERRAZANO (1485?–1528?) Italian navigator with whom Cartier first sailed; first European to see the bays of New York and Narragansett

Want to Know More?

At the Library

Harmon, Daniel. *Jacques Cartier and the Exploration of Canada*. Broomall, Penn.: Chelsea House, 2000.

Humble, Richard. *Voyages of Jacques Cartier*. New York: Franklin Watts, 1993.

On the Web

Discoverers Web: Jacques Cartier
http://www.win.tue.nl/~engels/discovery/cartier.html
Biography of Cartier along with important links

The Explorers: Jacques Cartier
http://www.vmnf.civilization.ca/explor/carti_e1.html
Details of Cartier's voyages

School Net: Jacques Cartier
http://geonames.nrcan.gc.ca/english/schoolnet/nfld/jacques.html
Brief biography of Cartier

■

Through the Mail

National Archives of Canada
395 Wellington Street
Ottawa, Ontario K1A 0N3
Canada
For historical information about Cartier and Canada

On the Road

The Mariners' Museum
100 Museum Drive
Newport News, VA 23606
757/596-2222
To see exhibits about navigators and sailors of all kinds

Index

About the Author

Jean F. Blashfield has worked for publishers in Chicago, Illinois, and Washington, D.C. A graduate of the University of Michigan, she has written more than ninety books, most of them for young people. Jean F. Blashfield has two adult children and lives in Delavan, Wisconsin.